Alphabet Zoo
Animals from A to Z

Written by Nancy Wolcott | Illustrated by Suzy Mellott

Copyright © 2021 by Nancy Wolcott and Suzy Mellott
ISBN: 978-0-578-34623-6
All rights reserved. This book, or parts thereof, may not be reproduced
in any form without written permission from the author and illustrator.
Library of Congress Cataloging-in-Publication Data is on file with the Library of Congress

Aa A is for Alpaca.

Alpacas have coats that are soft and furry.
They live on farms and they seldom hurry.
They hum and they shriek, they eat grass and leaves.
They'll carry your bags if you say, "Pretty please!"

Bb

B is for Bear.

Bears don't talk, though they often say "Grrr."
They're really quite large, and have brown or black fur.
They can climb trees and they like to fish.
A trout or a salmon is a bear's favorite dish.

Cc C is for Cat.

"Meow" says the cat, "mew" says a kitten.
They like being petted, they're soft as a mitten.
They snooze on the sofa or sleep on a bed.
A cat will adore you if you scratch its head.

Dd D is for Dog.

Dogs come in all sorts of shapes and sizes.
They'll follow commands if you give them prizes.
They love to play "catch" and go for a walk.
When a doggie says, "Woof", he's trying to talk!

Ee

E is for Elephant.

Elephants live for many years.
They have long trunks and big floppy ears.
They live in India, Africa too.
But the best way to see one is to go to a zoo.

Ff

F is for Fox.

The coat of a fox can be silver or red.
Her tail is quite fluffy, she has a slim head.
The young are called "kits" and are cute as can be.
They live in dens and don't climb a tree.

Gg

G is for Goat.

Goats live on mountains but also on farms.
They have hairy legs, but never have arms.
Goats can be milked and their cheese is quite yummy.
A baby says "baa" when it wants its mummy.

Hh H is for Horse.

Horses can trot, they jump fences and race.
A horse has a mane and a long narrow face.
A saddle and bridle are useful if you
Want to go for a ride? May I come too?

Ii

I is for Ibis.

His legs are long, his beak turns down.

He eats tiny crabs and looks like a clown.

He lives in the wetlands and nests in a tree.

If he sees a big gator, he'll take off and flee.

Jj

J is for Jaguar.

He looks like a panther; he's the biggest of cats.
He lives in warm climates and and eats coatis and rats.
His tail has black stripes and his jaws are so strong.
If you see him approaching, just say "So long!"

Kk

K is for Koala.

A koala's not a bear, the kangaroo is its cousin.
She loves eucalyptus leaves and eats them by the dozen.
She sleeps most of the day and is quite a slouch.
She carries her babies in a warm furry pouch.

Ll

L is for Lion.

The lion is called the king of the beasts.
He's very ferocious and not scared in the least.
He lives with a group that is called a pride,
And snoozes on rocks with his cubs by his side.

Mm

M is for Mule.

A mule's dad is a donkey. His mom is a horse.
He's speedy and smart, but you knew that, of course.
He hauls packs on his back, going up and down hills,
And the sound of his braying will sure give you chills!

Nn   N is for Narbalek.

What is a nabarlek? I didn't know, do you?
He's tiny and shy, and looks like a 'roo.
He's a kind of rock wallaby and swims all about,
And keeps getting new teeth when the old ones fall out.

Oo O is for Owl.

An owl's head can turn almost all the way around.
Her wings, when she's flying, don't make any sound.
Her eyes don't move, but she has great vision.
Feeding mice to her young is her full time mission.

Pp

P is for Pig.

A pig has a long nose, it's called a snout.
He lives in a sty where he wallows about.
He covers his body with mud to stay cool.
If a pig is your pet, he might swim in your pool!

Qq

Q is for Quail.

A quail is a bird who walks all around.
She lays ten to twelve eggs in her nest on the ground.
She flies south in the fall for her winter vacation.
On her head is a feather topknot, which is quite a sensation!

Rr

R is for Rabbit.

A rabbit has soft fur and a cute nose that wiggles.
Her strange way of hopping will give you the giggles!
Boy rabbits are called bucks, girls are called does.
When a rabbit is running, she runs on her toes.

Ss

S is for Sloth.

A sloth is an animal that doesn't get stressed.
She's a very strong swimmer, it's what she does best.
She sleeps upside down almost all day.
She's got a nice life, that's what I'd say!

T t

T is for Tiger.

Tigers are found in India and China.
With their orange & black stripes, there's no cat that's finer.
They live in the forest where they hunt for their prey.
Moms have two or three cubs, and they follow her all day.

Uu

U is for Urial.

If you like sheep with big horns, there's no denial,
You'll love this one, who's called a urial.
West Central Asia is the place she calls home.
On long grassy slopes she often does roam.

Vv

V is for Vulture.

This bird is nature's picker-upper.
He eats dead animals for his supper.
He has no feathers on the top of his head.
He's not very pretty, or so it's been said.

Ww W is for Walrus.

The walrus has tusks that are three feet long.
He's big, filled with blubber and his flippers are strong.
He lives on the rocks with a big group of friends,
And munches on clams as the daylight ends.

Xx

X is for X-ray Tetras.

The tetras are shiny, they're also quite slim.
You can see through their skin as they shimmer & swim.
They love to eat insects, their favorites are worms.
If you pick up a tetra, watch out as it squirms!

Yy

Y is for Yak.

If you're in Tibet and need help with your pack,
Just find a sherpa and he'll load up a yak.
Yak butter plus milk and some salt makes thick teas,
That help in cold weather so the sherpas don't freeze.

Zz

Z is for Zebra.

She looks like a horse, but won't let you ride.
Her coat has black and white stripes, side-by-side.
She lives in a herd on the African plains,
And migrates to find water before the spring rains.

And God said, "Let the waters bring forth swarms of living creatures,
and let birds fly above the earth across the dome of the sky."
So God created the great sea monsters and every living creature that moves,
of every kind, with which the waters swarm, and every winged bird of every kind.

And God said, "Let the earth bring forth living creatures of every kind:
cattle and creeping things and wild animals of the earth of every kind." And it was so.
God made the wild animals of the earth of every kind, and cattle of every kind,
and everything that creeps upon the ground of every kind.
And God saw that it was good.

—The New Oxford Annotated Bible